The Narrow *and* The Broad Way

Omie Mills, M.D.

Illustrations by John Fraser

Copyright © 2016 Omie Mills, M.D.
Copyright © 2016 TEACH Services, Inc.
ISBN-13: 978-1-4796-0556-9 (Paperback)
ISBN-13: 978-1-4796-0557-6 (iBooks)
ISBN-13: 978-1-4796-0558-3 (Kindle Fire)
Library of Congress Control No: 2016908696

TEACH Services, Inc.
P U B L I S H I N G
www.TEACHServices.com • (800) 367-1844

Young Johnny Miles,
A thoughtful lad,
Was learning to make choices,
Deciding good from bad.

One evening at worship
His Mom read a text,
"The narrow way leads to life
But the broad way
    leads to death."

"What does that mean?"
Johnny asked with concern.
This was a Bible truth
He wanted to learn.

"Where is the narrow way?
And where is the broad?
The path to life
Is the one I want to be on."

Mom settled down
In her big comfy chair
And began to explain
The "what" and the "where."

"These paths are not found
In one certain spot.
No such places will be marked
On a map with a dot.

"These paths are a picture
For our imagination
To help us see where we're headed...
To which destination.

"One way leads to life,
The other way to death.
Jesus gives us the Bible
So we don't have to guess.

"Now using our mind's eye
And our Bibles as maps,
Let's study the two roads
To get on the right path.

"First consider the broad road,
  Smooth, paved, and wide.
  Here you can walk as you wish
  For you are your own guide.

"For this reason most folks
  Travel this way,
  Free of laws or restrictions
  They have to obey.

"Rumor has it you're right
  To please only yourself
  No matter the cost
  To family, friends, or health.

"Here, happiness is planning
  The next fun thing to do
  Without thinking of others,
  Some poor, sick, and without food.

"And so they consider
  Only things they'll enjoy
  And try to find peace
  In amusements and toys.

"'What clothes should I wear
To impress my friends?
My TV show comes on soon.
I must watch it again!

"'Let's go to the theme park.
Have you seen that new movie?
Check out my video games!
This music is groovy!!'

"These travelers do
what feels good
Without thinking about
what's lost (like health).
They say 'MY body is
for MY use...
I am MY own boss.

"'I will eat what I want.
Don't tell me I can't.
Don't be so strict!
Just have fun!' they chant.

"Others think that happiness
Comes with lots of cash.
So they work from dawn till dusk;
Hurriedly they dash.

"Money! Money! Money!
There is never quite enough.
Soon every moment's filled
With cares, and work, and stuff.

"These travelers find interests
To which they must tend
And neglect to take notice
Where the broad road ends.

"The Bible sits dusty
On shelves in their homes.
'We're too busy to read it
Just now,' they moan.

"But neglecting the Bible
Is not wise.
It's like traveling blind
And following lies.

"And yet God reaches out
With Bible teachings as His voice,
Urging all who will listen
To make a better choice.

"Some will heed the warning
And choose the narrow route.
'Look out for death ahead!'
To broad road travelers they will shout.

"But many will think
To put off till later
A decision for God
And eternal matters.

"And so in not choosing,
They make a mistake
And at the end of the broad road
Too late they awake.

"'But wait! I'm not ready!'
They cry in dismay.
'If only I'd listened
And chosen the narrow way!'"

Johnny's mother replied,
"It's sad, I know,
To watch others travel
down the wrong road.

"But we can decide,
Unlike many others,
To follow Christ's leading
And give warning to others.

"Wow!" exclaimed Johnny
As he listened to Mom intently.
"Let's find the narrow way
And get on it quickly!"

"The narrow way is rugged
And often hard to find
Unless you follow God's Word
And keep the Bible in your mind.

"Study to know the Bible (2 Chronicles 20:20)
And His prophets' sayings too.
Safely you will walk
In all you say and do.

"To stay on the narrow way,
To avoid earth's distractions,
Study Philippians 4:8
And follow God's instructions.

"Think on the pure,
The noble, and true.
Talk of things lovely,
And praiseworthy too.

"Avoid the unclean,
The unkind, and hateful.
Love your neighbor well
And to God be grateful.

YOU SHALL HAVE NO
OTHER GODS BEFORE
ME.

YOU SHALL NOT MAKE
IDOLS.

YOU SHALL NOT TAKE
THE NAME OF THE
LORD YOUR GOD IN
VAIN.

REMEMBER THE SAB-
BATH DAY, TO KEEP IT
HOLY.

HONOR YOUR FATHER
AND YOUR MOTHER.

YOU SHALL NOT
MURDER.

YOU SHALL NOT
COMMIT ADULTERY.

YOU SHALL NOT
STEAL.

YOU SHALL NOT
BEAR FALSE WIT-
NESS AGAINST
YOUR NEIGHBOR.

YOU SHALL NOT
COVET.

"Because you love Jesus
You will trust He knows best
And will avoid sinful pleasures
And the things God detests.

"When choosing what to drink
And the foods that we should eat,
In caring for our minds and bodies
God's standards we will want to meet.

"Be generous and thoughtful.
Follow Jesus where He goes.
Put yourself aside as He did.
Tend to others' needs and woes

"And you will store up treasures
Where moths and mold
  will not corrupt.
Instead of keeping,
  give some more.
Still you'll find you have enough.

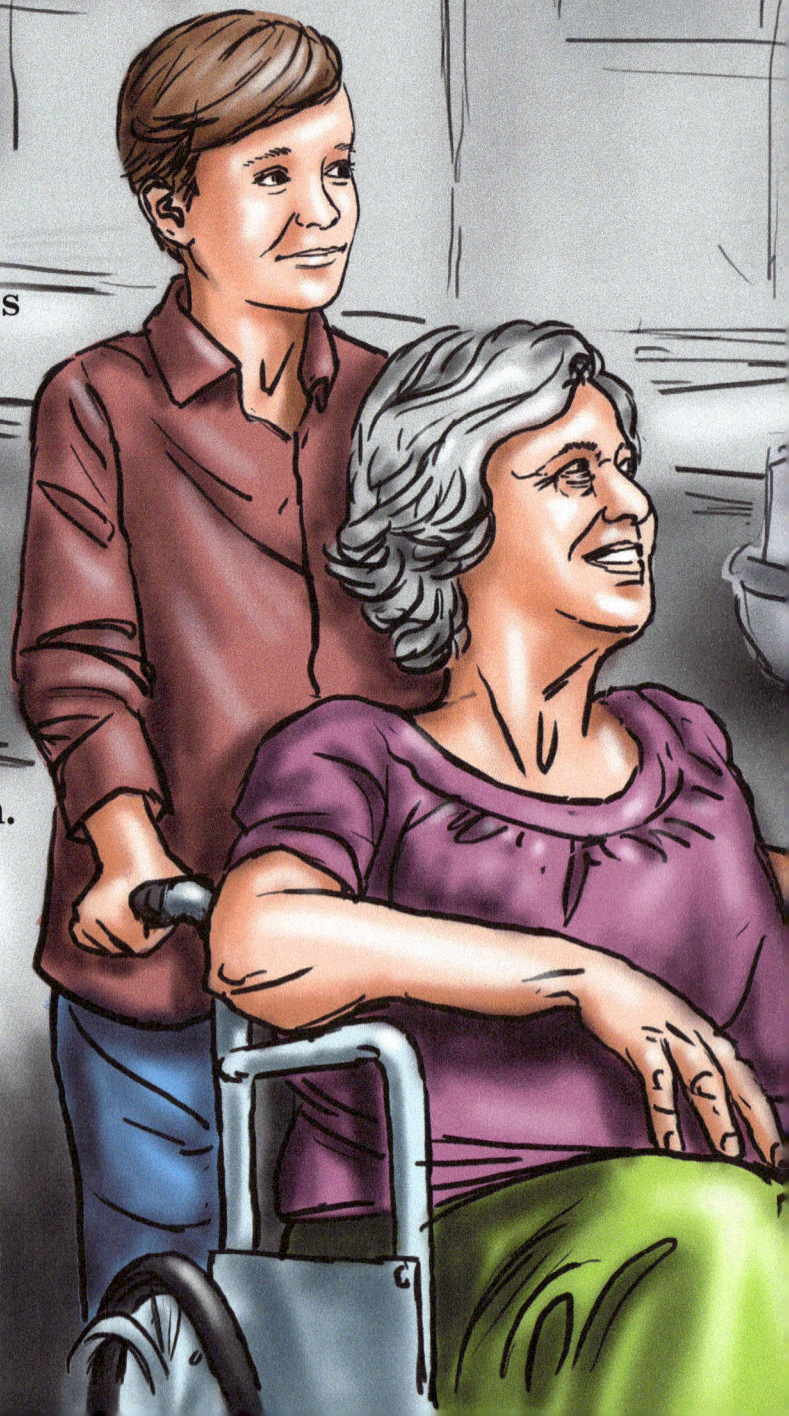

"Your daily choices
Will determine your way.
Will you live for yourself
Or choose God today?

"So take time every day
To read your Bible and to pray
And Jesus Christ will lead you
Along the narrow way.

"And when you come
To the end of this road
In happiness and joy,
You'll 'reap what you sow.'

"'Heaven's cheap enough!'
You'll shout with delight
And thank God for salvation
And the power to do right."

Then Johnny prayed, "Thank You, Jesus,
My very best Friend,
Because of Your love for me
I can have a great end.

"But that won't be all,
When on the narrow way I walk.
Soon I'll live with You in heaven
Where face-to-face we'll talk."

"And Mother, thank you
For sharing the Bible with me,
For teaching me God's way
Each night when we read.

"And just as you've taught me
Let's tell others this too
So all can get on the right path...
It's the narrow way we should choose!"

Said Johnny's Mother, "I'm glad...
To see you've got the picture
Of the narrow and the broad ways
And of who will be the victors.

"Trust and obey
    God's Word, the Bible.
    Follow Jesus' way
    And you'll stay on the right path
        Through each and every day."

We invite you to view the complete
selection of titles we publish at:

www.TEACHServices.com

Scan with your mobile
device to go directly
to our website.

Please write or email us your praises, reactions, or
thoughts about this or any other book we publish at:

info@TEACHServices.com

TEACH Services, Inc.
P U B L I S H I N G

TEACH Services' titles may be purchased in bulk for
educational, business, fund-raising, or promotional use.
For more information, please e-mail:

BulkSales@TEACHServices.com

Finally, if you are interested in seeing
your own book in print, please contact us at:

publishing@TEACHServices.com

We would be happy to review your manuscript for free.